SCHOLASTIC discover more™

Animal Babies

By Andrea Pinnington
and Tory Gordon-Harris

How to discover more

Animal Babies is specially planned to help you discover more about how animals are born and thrive.

Big words and pictures introduce an important subject.

Picture sequences show what happens in detail.

Small words help you explore pictures for active reading.

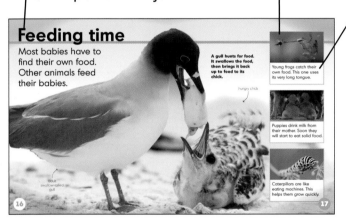

Feeding time

Most babies have to find their own food. Other animals feed their babies.

A gull hunts for food. It swallows the food, then brings it back up to feed to its chick.

hungry chick

Young frogs catch their own food. This one uses its very long tongue.

Puppies drink milk from their mother. Soon they will start to eat solid food.

adult swallow-tailed gull

Caterpillars are like eating machines. This helps them grow quickly.

Glossary

Index

The glossary explains words; the index helps you find them.

Digital companion book

Download your free all-new digital book, **Animal Babies Fun!**

Log on to
www.scholastic.com/ discovermore

Enter your unique code
RMP4WRK4WGX4

Fun animal activities

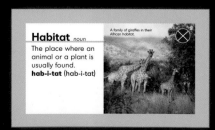

More animal words

Contents

Literacy Consultant: Barbara Russ, 21st Century Community Learning Center Director for Winooski (Vermont) School District

Natural History Consultant: Kim Dennis-Bryan

Library of Congress Cataloging-in-Publication Data Available

ISBN 978-0-545-36568-0

10 9 8 7 6 5 4 3 2 1   12 13 14 15 16

Printed in Singapore   46
First edition, March 2012

Who has babies?

All animals can have babies. The babies then grow up to become adults.

Animal facts

All animals can have babies.

All animals eat and breathe.

All animals move and can sense the world around them.

All animals grow.

orangutan, a type of ape

The circle of life

This baby ape has just been born.

He grows and becomes an adult.

Animals have babies. They grow up. They have babies of their own.

He gets older. Apes can live as long as 50 years.

He finds a mate. They have a family of their own.

Hatching

Most animals lay eggs. Baby animals grow inside the eggs.

A female ostrich lays its eggs on the ground.

Crack!

An ostrich chick begins to hatch.

It takes a long time for the chick to push its way out of the egg.

Inside an egg

A baby grows slowly inside an egg. It feeds on the yolk. When it is ready, it hatches.

hard shell

yolk

developing ostrich baby

The chick's feathers start to dry out and become fluffy.

Slowly, the chick stands up. It's ready to join its parents.

How many?

Egg-laying animals usually have more babies than animals that give birth to their young do.

mother

calf

1 A whale gives birth to one calf at a time.

2 A sheep usually gives birth to one or two lambs.

twin lambs

5 Many ducks lay five eggs at once. They hatch into ducklings.

fluffy ducklings

10 Geckos lay about ten eggs, which take six to eight weeks to hatch.

baby geckos

1000s Salmon lay lots of eggs. Some will survive to hatch into fry.

salmon fry

salmon eggs

Growing up

Some baby animals don't look like their parents. They change a lot as they grow.

green tree python

A chick slowly loses its fluff and gets feathers like its mom.

A cicada sheds its skin as it turns into an adult.

After a month, a baby panda is black, white, and furry like its mom.

These bright red and yellow tree pythons turn green as they get older.

Changes

Some animals change completely as they grow. This is called metamorphosis.

monarch butterfly

A female butterfly looks for a place to lay its eggs.

From egg to adult

The butterfly lays its eggs on a leaf.

egg

A caterpillar hatches out of each egg.

adult

This is the life cycle of a butterfly.

caterpillar

The adult butterfly breaks out of the pupa.

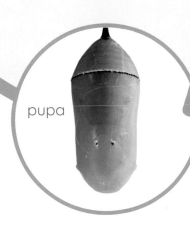
pupa

Each caterpillar builds a case called a pupa. The adult forms inside it.

That's my home

Some animals make homes for their babies. The home may be a nest, a burrow, or a pouch.

joey

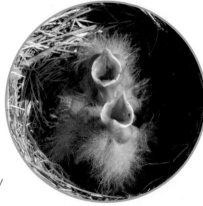

Beavers use wood to build dams in rivers. Their watery homes are called lodges.

This marsupial baby lives inside a pouch on its mother's tummy.

Birds build homes called nests. They raise chicks inside the nests.

Moles live underground.

baby mole
pup

**Moles live in burrows.
Their families stay safe
and warm underground.**

termite

Some animals live in
large homes called
mounds. This mound
was made by termites.

Feeding time

Most babies have to find their own food. Other animals feed their babies.

adult swallow-tailed gull

A gull hunts for food. It swallows the food, then brings it back up to feed to its chick.

hungry chick

Young frogs catch their own food. This one uses its very long tongue.

Puppies drink milk from their mother. Soon they will start to eat solid food.

Caterpillars are like eating machines. This helps them grow quickly.

Getting around

Animals have different ways of moving their babies from one place to another.

Baby scorpions catch a ride!

baby opossums

Baby opossums often travel on mom for food-gathering trips.

A mountain lion carries a cub gently in its jaws. It doesn't hurt the cub.

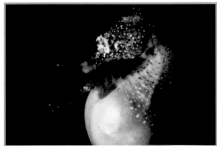

A male sea horse carries eggs in a pouch until they hatch.

Minutes after being born, a zebra foal can walk all by itself.

Lessons

Baby animals have to learn the skills they will need to survive as adults.

wolf pup

Play fighting with their brothers and sisters helps prepare wolf pups for adult life.

This wolf pup's mom teaches it how to hunt, howl, fight, and stay clean.

protective mom

It takes two to three years for a wolf pup to become an adult.

healthy pup

The mother wolf licks its newborn pup. The pup will soon learn to clean itself.

The mother wolf teaches the pups to howl. Wolves also learn to bark and whimper.

The small pup runs with its mom. The mother helps it learn how to hunt in the wild.

Babysitters

Like humans, some animals may get others to help them look after their babies.

dolphin pod

In a dolphin pod, or group, one male or female acts as an "aunt" or "uncle" to each calf.

These animals also use babysitters.

Male ostriches often take care of the eggs of up to five females.

Meerkats take turns babysitting their youngsters.

Crocodile hatchlings group together in crocodile nurseries.

Elephant calves are cared for by the whole herd.

baby bats

Baby bat pups huddle together for warmth in bat nurseries.

Journeys

Some baby animals have to travel far away from the places they were born.

Seals have their pups on land. The pups then travel out to the ocean.

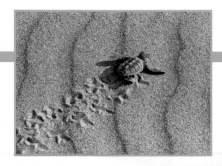

A baby turtle crawls down to the ocean after hatching in the sand.

Some salmon are born in rivers. Then they swim out to the ocean.

A wildebeest calf follows its mother for miles in search of grass.

sleeping
seal pup

Staying alive

Parents must take special care of their babies in extreme places.

Polar bears

Polar bears live in the freezing cold. A mother polar bear gives birth to its cubs in a snow den to protect them from the cold.

Spider monkeys

A spider monkey lives high up in the trees. It carries its baby around for two years. Then the baby climbs on its own.

A polar bear cub cuddles up to its mother's thick fur to stay warm.

Sandgrouse

Water is hard to find in the desert. A sandgrouse carries water to its chicks on its breast feathers.

chick

Mountain goats

A mountain goat mother stays below its kid. This keeps the kid from falling off the mountain edge.

Baby names

A baby deer is called a fawn. Other animals have special baby names, too.

deer

fawn

Can you think of any other baby animal names?

What are these babies called?

lion
cub

pigeon
squabs

hatchling
turtle

hedgehog
hoglet

swan
cygnets

kangaroo
joey

fish
fry

rabbit
kitten

whale
calf

Glossary

Burrow
An underground home dug by some animals, such as rabbits and moles.

Calf
The young of some animals, such as cows, whales, and elephants.

Caterpillar
A stage in the life cycle of a butterfly or moth.

Cub
The young of some animals, such as big cats and bears.

Desert
An extremely dry place.

Egg
A round or oval object laid by some female animals, such as birds, insects, and fish. A baby grows inside an egg.

Fry
The term for some small or newly hatched fish.

Hatch
To break out of an egg.

Hatchling
A newly hatched animal.

Life cycle
The stages of life that an animal goes through.

Marsupial
A type of animal, such as kangaroos and koalas, that often carries its young in a pouch on its stomach.

Metamorphosis
The big changes that happen to some animals as they grow from baby to adult.

Nest
A small home made by a bird or other animal.

Nursery
A place where a group of baby animals gathers together for warmth or for safety.

Pouch
A pocket on the front of some animals, in which they carry their young.

Pup
The young of some animals, such as seals and wolves.

Pupa
The hard case from which a butterfly or moth emerges.

Index

Thank you

Art Director: Bryn Walls
Designer: Ali Scrivens
Managing Editor: Miranda Smith
US Editor: Beth Sutinis
Cover Designer: Natalie Godwin
DTP: John Goldsmid
Visual Content Editor: Diane Allford-Trotman
Executive Director of Photography, Scholastic: Steve Diamond

Photography credits
1: Jenny E. Ross/Corbis; 3cl, 3r: iStockphoto; 4 (background), 4tl (pelican), 4tc (cow), 4bc (eye), 4bl (snails): iStockphoto; 4c (baby ape): Life on White/Alamy; 5t (ape with baby): Corbis Premium RF/Alamy; 5cl (older ape): Boris Diakovsky/Alamy; 5cr (swinging ape): Tim Jenner/Shutterstock; 5b (ape pair): Frans Lanting/Corbis; 6cl (large egg on hand): iStockphoto; 6c (nest): Karl Ammann/Getty Images; 6–7b (hatching sequence): Jane Burton/NPL; 7c (cross section): David Anthony/Alamy; 8 (whale and calf): Peter Chadwick/Getty Images; 9tl (sheep and lambs): Eric Isselée/Shutterstock; 9tr (ducklings): iStockphoto; 9c (geckos): Pan Xunbin/Shutterstock; 9b (eggs): Frans Lanting/Corbis; 9br (fry): Photoshot Holdings Ltd/Alamy; 10–11 (background): Szefei/Shutterstock; 10 (python): Martin Harvey/Alamy; 10 (branch): Gillmar/Shutterstock; 11tl (hen and chick): Eric Isselée/Shutterstock; 11tc (cicada): IrinaK/Shutterstock; 11tr (baby panda): Reuters/Corbis; 11tr (adult panda): Eric Isselée/Shutterstock; 11c (red python): Brad Thompson/Shutterstock; 11cr (yellow python): David Northcott/Corbis; 12c (butterfly on flower): Amana Images Inc./Alamy; 12b (butterfly on leaf): Nikola Bilic/Alamy; 13tr (butterfly on hand): Brberrys/Shutterstock; 13c (egg on leaf): iStockphoto; 13cl (flying butterfly): Ambient Ideas/Shutterstock; 13cr (caterpillar): Captainflash/iStockphoto; 13b (pupa): bhathaway/Shutterstock; 14–15 (mole in burrow): Tony Evans/Timelaps/Getty Images; 14bl (beaver dam): Tom Uhlman/

Alamy; 14bcl (joey): Hugh Lansdown/Shutterstock; 14br (chicks in nest): Wolfgang Zintl/Shutterstock; 15t (baby mole): iStockphoto; 15bl (termite mound): EcoPrint/Shutterstock; 15bfl (termite): Pan Xunbin/Shutterstock; 16–17 (gull and chick): Corbis RF/Alamy; 17t (frog): Buddy Mays/Corbis; 17c (puppies): Ocean/Corbis; 17b (caterpillar): Petrov Anton/Shutterstock; 18–19 (opossum and babies): Frank Lukasseck/Getty Images; 19tl (scorpion and babies): Scott Camazine/Alamy; 19tr (mountain lion): Robert Lindholm/Visuals Unlimited/Corbis; 19cr (sea horse): Rudie Kuiter/SeaPics; 19br (zebras): Elizevh/Shutterstock; 20 (pups playing): Arco Images GmbH/Alamy; 20tr (pup lying down): Eric Isselée/Shutterstock; 21tr (mother wolf): John Pitcher/iStockphoto; 21c (wolf pup): Eric Isselée/Shutterstock; 21bl (mother licking pup): Blickwinkel/Alamy; 21bc (mother howling and pup): Robert Pickett/Corbis; 21br (mother running with pup): Tom Brakefield/Corbis; 22–23 (dolphin pod): Martin Strmiska/Alamy; 23tc (ostrich eggs): Martin Bech/Shutterstock; 23tr (meerkats): AnetaPics/Shutterstock; 23bl (crocodiles): Reuters/Corbis; 23bc (elephants): Four Oaks/Shutterstock; 23br (bat hanging): EMprize/Shutterstock; 23br (bat group): Zolran/Shutterstock; 24–25 (seal pups): Momatiuk-Eastcott/Corbis; 25tl (baby turtle): Benjamin Albiach Galan/Shutterstock; 25tc (salmon): Natalie Fobes/Corbis; 25tr (wildebeest): iStockphoto; 26l (polar bear cubs): Jenny E. Ross/Corbis; 26r (spider monkeys): Nick Gordon/NPL; 27t (polar bear and cub): Frans Lanting Studio/Alamy; 27l (sandgrouse and chick): Peter Johnson/Corbis; 27r (goat and kid): National Geographic Stock; 28 (deer and fawn): Anan Kaewkhammul/Shutterstock; 29tl (lion and cub): Mogens Trolle/Shutterstock; 29tc (pigeon): Soleg/Shutterstock; 29tc (squab): Jovan Svorcan/Shutterstock; 29tr (turtle and hatchling): Paleka/Shutterstock; 29cl (hedgehog and hoglet): First Light/Alamy; 29c (swan and cygnet): iStockphoto; 29cr (kangaroo and joey): Smileus/Shutterstock; 29bl (fish): WILDLIFE GmbH/Alamy; 29bl (fry): Tsuneo Nakamura/Volvox Inc/Alamy; 29bc (rabbit and kitten): iStockphoto; 29br (whale and calf): Michael Patrick O'Neill/Alamy; 30–31: Tony Evans/Timelaps/Getty Images.

Cover credits
Front tl (praying mantis): Jeff R. Clow/Getty Images; tr (hanging ape): Eric Isselée/iStockphoto; c (background lion image): Richard du Toit/NPL; c (lion cub): Eric Isselée/iStockphoto. Back (elephants): Andy Rouse/NPL.